COME ON VICTORIA! I'M DONE.

Rantings about Melbourne's record-breaking days in lockdown

Elsie Johnstone
Graeme Johnstone

Come On Victoria! I'm Done.

Copyright © 2021 by Elsie Johnstone, Graeme Johnstone

Published by G. & E. Johnstone.

978-0-6453209-0-9

All rights reserved. No part of this publication may be reproduced in any manner whatsoever, or stored in a retrieval system or transmitted in any form or by any means, electronic, mechanical, photocopying, recording or otherwise, without the prior written permission of the author, except in the case of brief quotations embodied in critical articles or reviews. Please do not participate in or encourage the piracy of copyrighted materials in violation of authors' rights. Purchase only authorized editions.

The publisher and author assume no responsibility or liability whatsoever on the behalf of any purchaser or reader of this material. Any perceived slight of specific people or organizations is unintentional. While all attempts have been made to verify information provided in this publication, neither the author nor the publisher assumes any responsibility for errors, omissions or contrary interpretation of the subject matter herein.

Come On Victoria, I'm Done is also available as an e-book for Kindle, Kobo, Apple and other devices.

Foreword

IT is not much fun being confined to four walls for 263 days.

In the beginning, Australia was seen as the world's pin-up nation for dealing with the COVID spread. But keeping cases and deaths down to a handful compared to the spiralling statistics of the US and Europe came at a heavy mental and physical cost for its citizens.

In a period of 20 months from March 2020 to November 2021, Victorian Premier Daniel Andrews called six lockdowns.

The first was a botched hotel quarantine that killed 800 people. After that he was running scared and any sudden burst, even of just two or three cases, was reason enough for him to hit the panic button and push everybody back indoors.

Schools, businesses, services, community groups, even virus-free rural communities hundreds of kilometres from the capital city, all copped the brunt of it.

There were a few exceptions, largely those sectors involving the unions that supported his government, along with racing, football and brothels.

Aggravating the situation, the national race to fix the problem morphed into a vanity contest between the six State Premiers and the Prime Minister, Scott Morrison, as a line-up of inflated political egos paraded at the remorseless daily press conferences. It wasn't all about health advice.

The states took it in turn to blame each other, while national leadership was found wanting. This was particularly so in the rollout of the 'it's not a race' vaccine campaign, which turned into a monumental shambles.

The finger pointing between traditional rivals Victoria and New South Wales was fired up even further by Morrison describing NSW's test-and-trace strategy as the 'gold standard'.

In turn, Andrews blamed cases leaking into Victoria on the then NSW Premier Gladys Berejiklian, as well as three Sydney furniture removalists and a Bondi limousine driver.

Ultimately Melbourne set a new world lockdown record.

For the innocent bystander it was frustrating to have the goal posts moved every time freedom appeared to be on the horizon.

You can't confine the population to barracks for months on end and not expect burnout, frustration and anger.

Let us tell you about it.

Contents

By the numbers 2
Liminality 4
Dan's daily press conference 5
The one day that saves me 6
ANZAC day 2020 8
End of Lockdown Number 3 9
Exit to Rome 10
All part of the language 12
No fooling, a plan to save the day 14
Cleaning out the garage 16
Lockdown layabout lifer 18
Groundhog day 20
My beloved's scary admission 22
Lockdown Number 4 24
Fab Friday falls flat 25
What happens if ..? 28
To jab, or not to jab? 29
Pleading for a shot 30
Vaccine responses around the world 32
Lockdown Number 5 34
When the tennis players came to town 35
Government art of evading it all 36
Only one nation to save 38
Twenty days of footy heaven 40
Locked out of the sunshine 42
The Olympics in Tokyo 43
We're over it, Dan! 44
The new look Games 46
At last 47
The authors 48

COME ON VICTORIA! I'M DONE.

By the numbers

WHEN it came to being confined to quarters, residents of the State of Victoria became very practiced, with Premier Daniel Andrews ready to pull the lockdown trigger at the slightest hint of the virus spreading.

Six times he did that.

Ultimately, on Monday October 4, Melbourne set the record that no other metropolis envied. Reaching 246 days, it took over from the Argentinian capital of Buenos Aires as the city that had spent the most cumulative days under stay-at-home orders.

And there was more to come.

Come On Victoria! I'm Done.

It panned out like this:

- Lockdown 1: March 30, 11.59 pm, 2020 to May 12, 11.59 pm, 2020 (43 days).

- Lockdown 2: July 8, 11.59 pm, 2020 to October 27, 11.59 pm, 2020 (111 days).

- Lockdown 3: February 12, 11.59 pm, 2021 to February 17, 11.59 pm, 2021 (5 days).

- Lockdown 4: May 27, 11.59 pm, 2021 to June 10, 11.59 pm, 2021 (14 days).

- Lockdown 5: July 15, 11.59 pm, 2021 to July 27, 11.59 pm, 2021 (12 days).

- Lockdown 6: August 5, 2021, 8.00 pm, to October 21, 11.59 pm, 2021 (78 days).

The result? Victorians spent a combined 263 days in liminality.

Liminality? It's a state of transition between one stage of a person's life and the next. A sort of twilight zone, during which your social mobility, or your work situation, comes to a halt.

Liminality

Ours is a time of stillness, of time suspended
The world we once knew has been up and over-ended
We sit through this lockdown silent and ponderous
What happens after the virus, what is beyond us?
We have feelings of uncertainty, a need to make preparation
Unfamiliar landmarks light the way, and we fear dislocation
The past is gone, the present real, the future undefined
We reaffirm concepts held and our expectations redefine
In the stillness of this place in the space between spaces
We meet our new normal, time to pause, realign, embrace it
One thing we know, things will change for sure
We won't retrieve exactly what was, that will be no more
But like the caterpillar, we have no way of knowing
Whether changes we experience will be temporary or ongoing
How deep our transformation, what will happen in the cocoon
Will it be good or bad; will it happen soon?
There is beauty in liminality as we wait for life to transform us
Cross this bridge, take deep breaths, relax and allow it to form us
Live in the present as we await our destiny
Life is a series of changes, what will be, will be

- Elsie

Come On Victoria! I'm Done.

Dan's daily press conference

At eleven o'clock Dan leads the show at the COVID altar
The same daily sermon given by men drunk on power
Orders barked out loud and clear at this news conference hour
We'll tell you what we allow
We'll tell you when and how
We will say when the laws will ease
And when you can come and go as you please
Until then, there are only five reasons to be out
Plus a couple more that are discretionary
We grant exemptions for football, horse racing and brothels
To keep the men folk happy
But dancing is definitely unnecessary
And as tough as it sounds, kids in small apartments don't need playgrounds
So we will lock the women in their homes, schooling the kids, while they 'Keep that noise down!!'

But I'm telling you now, the more they disallow, the more anger will increase
Our freedoms have been stripped from us, we gave them up without a fuss
For the benefit of us all, an order tall, but enough is enough
Our frustration with our situation mounts day by day
But don't dare march in the streets to have your say
Because those who have done so were met with violence
Severely silenced
The police react whenever the two groups meet
With pepper balls and capsicum spray, and rubber bullets fired at speed
Large fines imposed because of orders they failed to heed
And taken to task for failure to wear a mask
While they voice their concern that the freedoms hard earned
Have been taken away
And the people have no say

- Elsie

The one day that saves me

I am just holding on in lockdown
Battling hard not to go under
I try not to think of the Ring of Steel
Or massive quarantine blunders

Or the daily set of COVID numbers
Fed to us granule by granule
Or the tired jacket and gloomy face
Of our introspective leader Daniel

I read everything I can get hold of
Until my eyes are blurred with dots
Papers and books, biogs of cooks
And the form guide for the Kilmore Trots

I play every board game that we have
Play every vinyl album on hi-fi
Fire up the cassette and CD players
And almost exhaust Spotify

But one thing makes it worthwhile
A job that makes my heart sing
I look forward to Thursday morning
When I can go and put out the bins

Yes, this is highlight of my week
My freedom-loving fun day
I get so excited about the whole idea
I start dreaming about it on Sunday

Come On Victoria! I'm Done.

Then on Monday I check the schedule
Which bin's turn is it for the week?
Is it time for Garry the Green Waste?
Or Recycling Roger to go on the street?

Plus, of course, Weekly Waste Wally
And, when the place is like a fall-out shelter
We diligently dig up the tough trash
For Harry The Hard Rubbish Helper

You can see what effect this has had on me
All good sense has been shot down in flames
You know the lockdown has warped your mind
When you start giving your rubbish bins names

So, what's the big deal, you are thinking
Why do I love such a mundane task?
Well, for a fleeting second I can stand in the street
Without wearing a flamin' mask …

- *Graeme*

ANZAC Day 2020

It's ANZAC Day in lockdown
Flying foxes in their riverside retreat the only sound
As houses slowly waken and there is stirring in our street
And we rise one by one to stand and commemorate
The brave men and women who have gone before
Who fought and died for our country in many a bloody war
Dogs bark, the neighbour's pet rooster crows
The first morning coffee brews, outside first light glows
Torches illuminate the dawn
ANZAC Service has come home
Young couple reverently places a candle on the kerb
From various houses young families emerge
A child proudly wearing war medals given long ago
To a man who has gone before that he didn't even know
An Australian flag proudly draped across the gate
A chalk-drawn soldier on the pavement of the house at number eight
Along the street faint glow of candles on the pavement
The simplicity of the gesture a sentimental statement
An old man wears his medals from the Vietnam war
His wife who stands by his side knows who he's crying for
Two nature-strip trees decorated with knitted poppies red
The crafty women completed that task before they went to bed
A breeze of muted whispers, as in the background
The distant buzz of motor cars, towards the city bound
The flat note of a child bugler in the light of a lamp post
Playing a delightfully imperfect version of the 'Last Post'
Two minutes of silence, a time for reflection
Some homemade wreaths laid with reverend circumspection
Then 'Reveille' and 'Lest We Forget
ANZAC Day in lockdown, so simple and yet
The sun rises
To another day in lockdown
Full of surprises

- Elsie

Come On Victoria! I'm Done.

End of Lockdown Number 3

Newfound freedom
The national lockdown's done
After endless isolation in our homes, now it's time for fun
Grab a haircut, go to the movies, spend our money in the stores
At long last, gyms, hotels and retail trade can open up their doors
Friends gather, strangers meet, acquaintances reunited
Enjoy a parma and pint at a pub
I'm excited
Families happily meet to share a meal, laugh and have fun
Conversation and laughter flows in the late afternoon sun
What do I wear? What do I say? It's been a long time
After more than a year of deprivation, we've been thrown a lifeline
Time to rediscover each other
Reconnect with one another
After months of isolation
Escaped at last from our prison
Nothing dulls the senses more
Than the permanent alarm we felt before
How I love the city life, dancing, hugs and laughter
Happy to be free again
This is the life we're after

- Elsie

Exit to Rome

Good evening, Sir
Welcome to Sydney airport
I see you are leaving for Rome

I'm just a bit confused
According to COVID rules
None of us are allowed to leave home

Unless of course
From the right source
You have a Government issued exemption

But from what I can see
You simply handed me
This note, 'My Flight to Redemption'

Still, I'll let you through
What on earth can I do?
Not for me to be all testy and flighty

No need for the PM to sign
Or a Minister on the line
When it reads, 'Okayed by The Almighty'

But I assure I'm not lying
Italy's COVID figures are rising
Smart Traveller warns you, do not visit

Plus the usual crime
And corruption all the time
A place where bad outweighs good, isn't it?

Come On Victoria! I'm Done.

What's that, sir?
You don't worry about these things
You don't care if they don't mask their faces

That you are a man of your own
Off to the Vatican throne
And have friends in the highest of places

Enjoy your flight, Sir.

             *- **Graeme***

All part of the language

Before 2020 there were words we did not know or say
Now they are part of the language, used each and every day
Who even knew what a pandemic was, before all this corona stuff started?
Was it the same as an epidemic, or were we in waters unchartered?
What did we know of Wuhan? Where is that? In China, dead-set in the middle?
Did the virus escape or did bats cause the total worldwide transmittal?
Our aim at first was to flatten the curve so hospitals could cope
Then politicians decided total eradication to be the one big hope
The enemy was droplets, sneezes, infected surfaces and everything in between
Now, apparently, it is carried in the air but luckily we have a vaccine
Had you ever heard of AstraZeneca or Pfizer?
What percentage efficacy? What is efficacy? Are epidemiologists any wiser?
Who, except health professionals, had ever heard of PPE?
Personal Protective Equipment
Put on your gear, wear a mask, the loudly applauded key
Keep a physical distance of 1.5 metres from people walking by
No visiting family or showing affection
Too bad if someone you love should die
Celebrations cancelled, funerals capped at ten, grievers left alone to cry, take it on the chin
We don't hear about petri dishes any more
But cruise liners have still been deleted from the score
Parents schooling their kids at home, stay away from friends, when will all this end?

Come On Victoria! I'm Done.

The future is out of our hands, not ours to plan,
live solely for today
No weddings, travel, celebrations, no weekend get away
People in lockdown, at home, sad and alone, vulnerable, depressed
and bedridden
All this you can cop, say the men at the top, take note what's
allowed and forbidden
Blood clots are not a worry
Get a vaccine, don't delay, hurry!
Our contact tracing team is really truly mean
Almost as effective as our hotel quarantine!

- Elsie

No fooling, a plan to save the day

He had lost his bronze tan
The Gold Coast tourist man
And his voice was trembling with unbridled fear

'We'll all hit the skids
'Now your Victorian school kids
'Aren't allowed to party-on up here this year!'

He said he couldn't go on
That the lockdown was wrong
And it was unfair a ban had been put on Schoolies

So, I've devised a plan
To help him out of his jam
I'm heading north with my group, The Old Foolies

We will be, without fail
At the other end of the scale
To join our group, you must be over seventy

So, we'll bring a full-time nurse
And our own private hearse
With a defibrillator in each room a necessity

And grab-handles on the showers
And please, no bloody flowers
Because the pollen will give us all a bout of sneezing

But, yes, cylinders of oxygen
And oodles of amoxicillin
To stop the flu, the coughing, and the wheezing

Come On Victoria! I'm Done.

Comfy beds for painful backs
Door hooks to hang cream slacks
Are a must, of course, for this veteran adventure

And can we stay near a Coles?
One that stocks Dr Scholls?
And Polident on special for our dentures?

There'll be no noise and fuss
Don't you worry about us
We have our games and some of them are corkers

Books for colouring in
Making picture frames out of tin
And who can stand longest without his walker

Oh, I know we're in lockdown
And the borders are in block down
But you can trust us, we're clever old commuters

We'll travel by the back roads
And emerge from the shadows
A mighty herd of souped-up mobility scooters

So, mate, just be patient
Don't be a complainant
Once we reach the 'Goldie' we'll ease your fiscal tension

Our Old Foolies revival
Will lead to your survival
When we head for the RSL after we collect our pension

— ***Graeme***

Cleaning out the garage

We've done all the household chores, thanks to the coronavirus
The windows are clean, the skirtings gleam, spiders downed from their cobwebs
The curtains are washed, the oven scrubbed, gone is the kitty litter
Floors are polished, silver rubbed,
so that it shines a light and bright glitter
Cupboards emptied and stacked neatly when cleaned
Not one speck of dust is to be seen
The house is so sparkling but it's only I that know it
I should ask the neighbours in, if only just to show it
I have watched everything and anything on Netflix
Taught the dog a handful of new tricks
Out in the garden, things look shipshape
I've planted out vegies and watch them take shape
The grass is green, the leaves raked up
Paths are so clean, weeds burnt up
The pool is pristine, I catch each leaf before it flutters
I've even had the ladder out and cleared all the gutters
With nothing more that I can do here
In staunch resolve and tremulous fear

Come On Victoria! I'm Done.

I open the garage door
Just one look says it all
I know that there's a car in there
I can't be exactly sure just where
There are tins of paint stacked high from years before
Bikes, I think I counted six or more
There are kiddies' toys from when men were boys
A three-wheeled pram brings back past joys
There's two or three stuffed boxes and all sorts of tape
Camping gear, six hessian bags, a black magician's cape
There's a pile of out-dated newspapers from when
the young lad did the round
I now understand why the newsagent ranted when
they could not be found
I stand and ponder this pile of shit
And wonder what I will do with it
Some of it is still quite good and I think aloud if I should
Put it all back and drive to Bunnings to buy more shelving
This task at hand is too overwhelming

- Elsie

Lockdown layabout lifer

Dear Premier Dan
My name is Stan
And your new rules I don't need to decipher

Cos, I'm stayin' inside
Not goin' out for a ride
I'm now a lockdown layabout lifer

It's great at home here
Having an ice cold beer
On the way to breakfast straight down the hall

It sets me up for the day
Once I've found an ashtray
For hours of doing sweet bugger all

Yes, I'm starting to pong
And my hair is so long
I look quite like that bloke they called Lennon

That is, the Commo hustler
Who took over Russia
And not the Beatle who said that there is no heaven

I'm a grumpy old bugger
Not a people hugger
Conversation is now something that I scoff

I grunt and I groan
And don't answer the phone
And maybe that's why the missus finally took off

Did she do a bolter!
I simply couldn't halt her
She departed one day, leaving no traces

Come On Victoria! I'm Done.

Yes, it was my blooper
Losing all our Super
Betting online on the Warrnambool races

So it's a bit of a battle
'Round the kitchen I rattle
Trying to live within my cheap means

But I've learnt a thing or two
It's amazing what you can do
With a gherkin and a can of sardines

- Graeme

Groundhog day

I've been locked up, locked down and locked up again
I'm a people person, so it goes against my grain
But Dan says, 'Stay home, work through the pain.'
Just to quote the old cliché
It's groundhog day
Again, again, again, the same

Stay inside, don't venture out, don't leave your floor
Nobody wants to talk any more
Me and my faithful Labrador
Watch statistics mount with dismay
It's groundhog day
Again, again, again, the same

Dan says it's not too much to ask
If you venture out, wear a mask
Stealthy figures slink silently past
A bad guy or good guy, I innocently ask?
Can't come out to play today
It's groundhog day
Again, again, again, the same

People dying, mourners crying
If this gets away, it will be terrifying
It's essential to have us all complying
People in the churches pray
It's groundhog day
Again, again, again, the same

Come On Victoria! I'm Done.

Stay at home, don't go far, immobilise us
Public shame, a huge fine, a dose of the virus
Police will check credentials
Allow us out to buy essentials
If we falter, we pay
It's groundhog day
Again, again, again, the same

Endless football on the TV
Sit outside in the sun and read
Empty the garden of every weed
Knit a jumper for Uncle John
Another six weeks, it goes on and on and on
In my home hideaway
It's groundhog day
Again, again, again, the same

Now it's all for one and one for all
Let's get this done, what are we waiting for?
Third time for real, this is all-out war
Vanish doomsday and groundhog day
If this lockdown proves a failure
Victoria will be the laughing stock of Australia

- Elsie

My beloved's scary admission

There was a long moment of silence
At this morning's breakfast table
As if all communication
Had suddenly been disabled

My beloved look unsettled
An empty screen on her phone
As she stared wanly around
Our otherwise empty home

Then she uttered these words
That cut me like a sword
Looking at me and intoning
'You know what? I'm bored!'

Oh, blimey, crikey, help me
I felt so utterly confused
I'd failed my lockdown role
Of keeping her amused

And interested and informed
And happy and entertained
And stretching out the limits
Of her magnificent, fertile brain

Had I not I started the day
With the newspaper trivia?
Then read aloud a piece about
An insurgency in Bolivia?

Come On Victoria! I'm Done.

'And listen to this, dear,' I said
'It'll be of long-term use
'Let me explain the difference
'Between Russia and Belarus.'

Undeterred, I played some music
But neither Country nor Pop
Alas, 'Moldovan Funeral Marches'
Only made her say, 'Please stop!'

That blocked me moving on
To Stravinsky and Tchaikovsky
While discussing the political merits
Of Lenin versus Trotsky

Wait! This'll spark things up
A topic that'll hit like a laser
'Hey darl, did I tell you of the time
'I met Malcolm Fraser ..?'

- *Graeme*

Lockdown Number 4

Just when we thought we could take no more
They've locked us up in Lockdown Number 4
Don't complain, politicians explain, it's just a small, small tweak
If you'd had the jab, it would be not be so bad, but for now stay home for a week
Don't blame faulty contact tracing or the vaccine rollout that needs replacing
There's one main reason alone for this failure
Just face the fact, and be very exact,
this virus escaped from South Australia
Don't complain, hunker down again and repeat
what we did this time last year
Relax, take it easy, we got this, it's breezy,
tune ourselves down to low gear
Fall out of bed when you like, take a hike, ride your bike,
or fiddle around with a hobby
Do as you please, you have no one to appease,
wear what you like on your body
Give the bathroom a scrub, ensuring it's clean,
sort the washing and set the machine
Do a quick search for odd socks, and discarded jocks,
throw them in with the wash to be cleaned
Choose a good book, find a nice sheltered nook,
sit out in the sun until it is done
Then hang it out to dry, keeping an eye on the sky,
a job well begun is half done
That's enough for one day, it's now time to play,
but there's nobody to go out play with
So I'm writing a poem, at home here alone,
and in doing so became a wordsmith
One can't help wondering that with all this bluff and blundering,
our leaders are leading us a merry dance
Just let us go free, leave us alone, let us be,
and allow us to weigh up our own chance

- Elsie

Come On Victoria! I'm Done.

Fab Friday falls flat

I'm feeling very patriotic
I'm ringing the civic bell
I'm doing my best for my city
Clawing back from lockdown hell

Bringing the buzz back
Is the latest Melbourne idea
'Fab Friday,' they've dubbed it
'An after-work wine or beer!'

It's a great COVID plan
To fill empty bars and stores
Especially with our kindly boss
Letting us get off work at four

'Go on, clear out,' he said
'Make those glasses clink
'But follow the golden rule
'Have only one cheeky drink!'"

So, there was a group of us
At the bar, gathered around
Soon joined by a lawyer
From Green, Blue and Brown

Plus some advertising chaps
And a couple of chums from school
Who spend the day trading shares
While still acting the fool

The property boys arrived
With several clients in tow
Plus four blokes from banking
Heading to the river for a row

We recalled the boss' advice
About not daring to overload
But then someone whispered
'How 'bout one for the road ..?'

From that moment on
Things get a little bit blurry
Explaining why my mouth's so dry
And my tongue is rough and furry

I have some vague memories
Of a stage full of strippers
And someone cutting my hair
With a pair of poodle clippers

And a big Kiwi bloke saying,
'Here, give this a good chew
'It'll take your mind off the pain
'While I finish your tattoo.'

And then Bruce from Finance
Got all hungry and narky
Until we calmed him down
With a street vendor souvlaki

Finally, the piece de resistance
To finish this crazy night
Someone loudly suggesting
'Who's up for a mystery flight?'

Come On Victoria! I'm Done.

Off we went to Qantas
And joined the back of a queue
But we ended up on Qatar Airlines
Well, they both start with a Q …

So now here I quietly lie
In my jocks and a feather boa
Handcuffed in an airport cell
In a faraway place called Doha

It'll be ages before we return
That's what authorities think
How I wish I'd stuck to the limit
Of just one cheeky drink

But, the lawyer is proving handy
As things follow their course
The papers lobbed this morning
And he's a specialist in divorce …

- Graeme

What happens if ..?

What happens if I'm not immunised?
Will I be scrutinized and criticised?
Doomed to be ostracised
Treated as an anti-Christ?

What if I show hesitation
To partake of the group immunisation
Of the entire nation
Will I be an aberration?
Deserve severe castigation?
Open myself to self-flagellation?

What if I choose to forego the jab
Until the scientists return to their lab
To rethink, redo and then unwrap
A better version, not a death trap?

What happens if I forsake
The opportunity to vaccinate
Diminishing the uptake rate
Preventing Australia from opening her gate?

Will other folk think me unsound?
Greet me with a knowing frown?
Deliver a thorough dressing-down?
Saying, 'Don't come near me
'Stay far away as you can be
'You impede our herd immunity.'

- Elsie

Come On Victoria! I'm Done.

To jab, or not to jab?

I admit to being part of a mild insurrection
A group that is quietly heading in an innocent direction
But enough to cause the Government to engage in our detection
To jab or not to jab? Now, that is our big question

We're shuffling old geezers, ranging from far and near
Still loving a glass of wine or a schooner of beer
But conscious of our health as the final curtain draws near
Why risk being finished off early? Now that's our real fear

We meet surreptitiously in bowls club parking lots
Or amid the beachside tea-tree in discreet talkative knots
Discussing the pros and cons of getting our COVID shots
With particular focus on the phrase "potential blood clots"

'Oh,' the docs say, 'that only applies to people under fifty
'It's just four in a million, and you are calling that risky?'
But we reckon that explanation sounds a bit of a swifty
This Government is renowned for being evasive and shifty

You never know how all this will pan out, now, do ya?
This synthetic crap could run, and run right through ya
And not just for a few days will it quietly subdue ya
But cause a thrombosis that could, um, finally screw ya

Even if not, you could get pain, chills, or swelling
That seems to be good enough reason for some yelling
And muscle soreness and headache? They sound rather telling
With nausea and fever requiring more medical quelling

Still, I guess, we should line up and do our duty
I would hate to be known as aloof and snooty
Even if the companies are adding to their sizeable booty
If I don't comply, this Government will either jail or shoot me

- *Graeme*

Pleading for a shot

Hello, Doc? Please pick up
I'm in a state of total abjection
I've been phoning and phoning and phoning all day
To book for my COVID injection

The website said to call you up
And state my case with accurate brevity
Well, I'm ready to go, got me muscles on show
I'm classified '1b', well over seventy

But you refuse to answer my call
Are you on your yacht? Or down at the farm?
It's not much to ask, a simple task
Just a quickie straight into me arm

See, I've worked hard for this country
Given it my heart and soul
Well, except for a momentary loss of mojo
Spending fourteen years on the dole

And, yes, there was that decade
When things got a little bit slack
But it's hard to do your best
With a bit of a twinge in your back

And, I do understand, dear Doctor
How I reduce you to tears
When I'm still on sixty ciggies a day
And enjoying my six-packs of beers

Come On Victoria! I'm Done.

And when I refuse to take on board
Your ideas on fitness, health and diet
Particularly as I won't eat any meal
Unless the missus has triple-fried it

Despite all that, dear Doctor
Please stop ignoring me
I pledge that I'm ready to follow
The Prime Minister's vaccine plea

But I insist on the shot made locally
Not some back-street vaccine subgenera
I know me jabs, I've been keeping tabs
What's it called, now? The Aspro Enema ..?

- Graeme

Vaccine responses around the world

Good evening, all!
I'm a good old English pensioner
Who's turned one hundred and six
And yesterday I had the virus jab
Just the second person on the list

It was the NHS what did it
Via a shot in my skinny old arm
'Tho I was dubious when the doctor said
'This won't do you no harm …'

They seem to be starting with us oldies
As a way of giving the vaccine a fly
I reckon they'll say if we all drop dead
'Well, it was certainly worth a try …'

Good mornink!
My name is Dimitri Alexander Tripov
And it is truly great to be alive
For in Mother Russia I was the first injected
With Sputnik Vaccine Number 5

A beautifully named miracle cure
The whole nation is so very proud
The minute they shoved it in my arm
I was rocketing up to the clouds

And now I am circling the earth
And talking to Moscow via the telly
And now I am passing over India
Is working! I can see Red Temple of Delhi!

Come On Victoria! I'm Done.

Hi, y'all!
I'm Jim Bob Junior from Georgia
And this here is my Colt 45
It sure is a handy little weapon
Over the years, it's kept me alive

So if a doc comes at me with a needle
He will have my pistol to evade
Along with my semi-auto rifle
And my rocket launcher, military grade

I figure this virus is a fraud
To subdue us tax-paying residents
If I want a cure, I'll take that hydroxy stuff
Like Donald, my favourite President

Ah, g'day!
I'm a tough old bugger from Australia
I wear long white socks playing bowls
Being the last man standing among my mates
Is at the top of my life-time goals

I don't wanna die before they do
I don't wanna give them even a hunch
That they'll one day dance on me grave
And go back to the club for lunch

So I am patiently biding my time
To see the effect of this rushed vaccine
And to gauge just how safe it is
I'll keep a very good eye on the Queen ...

- Graeme

Lockdown Number 5

God only knows how we will ever survive
Victoria's Lockdown Number 5
We went through Number 1 and when that was done
It was extended
Became open ended
Merged into Lockdown 2
What were we to do?
We were confined to home the whole winter long
We gritted our teeth and strove to be strong
Lockdown Number 3
Was much longer than we could ever foresee
We endured and saw it through
Found lots of different things to do
Vowed that we'd slay this virus
It would not get the better of us
We emerged at the other end
Vowed never to go there again
But come Valentine's Day and we had no say
Another lockdown, short and quick, a low price to pay
The politicians boasted, we have this virus roasted
The end song is freedom
The beast is beaten
They were wrong
But still they strung us along
There have been numerous mistakes, blunders and mess-ups
Pass the buck, lips are sealed, no one 'fessed up
It's making us glum
We are done, done, done
We have no more to give so let's agree to live and let live
Allow the virus run its course and fade away
We can all get back to work and school and play
Because there's nothing left but an empty bag of tricks
Time for our pollies to stop playing politics

- Elsie

Come On Victoria! I'm Done.

When the tennis players came to town

After we'd endured months of lockdown
The tennis players came to town
Expat Aussies were locked behind other country borders
Patiently waiting to be issued with orders
That allowed them to come home
To family and all that they own
But for the tennis players everything was fine
Big money, politics and sport apparently form a different paradigm
Seems the tennis circus is another matter entirely
Did the process involve bribery?
They somehow jumped the queue
What did they have to do?
Did politicians want us glued to our screens to distract and entertain us
Give us things to bet upon, forget that they detained us
That Aussie citizens were not allowed home, even if they could
While we were kept in our homes for the common good
How come players and their teams pushed our nationals aside?
For these kings and queens of the court why were rules simplified?
It doesn't seem fair
It doesn't seem right
But power and money speaks loud and clear, wins over our birthright.

- Elsie

Government art of evading it all

Hello, a warm welcome to EVADER
You are smart to sign up for this course
Whether a director, manager or secretary
In Health, or Government or the Force

With these darn Royal Commissions
Questioning, haranguing and sniping
No longer can you blame a balls-up on
'That nice little Greek girl in Typing'

At EVADER we are supremely skilled
At teaching tricks of public denial
No more, 'First that I've heard of this!'
Or, 'It's somewhere here in the pile'

EVADER is 'Educating Vacuous Administrators
To Deny Executive Responsibility'
Once you pass, you'll keep your post
No matter how modest your ability

First, a Diploma in Bobbing & Weaving
So they can't get a bead on you at all
Then, a Bachelor of Persuasiveness
To make a big problem sound small

Then a Masters in Mis-Communication
Explaining how your plan was dashed
When your e-mail inbox overfilled
Which made the NBN crash

Come On Victoria! I'm Done.

And not only that, your phone went flat
And your iPad fell behind the sofa
And your laptop was stolen by a homeless junkie
And you left your Fitbit at break-of-dawn yoga

They'll think you're healthy and spiritual
Although a bit of a digital oddball
So, we'll add a Doctor of Philosophy
Based on the thesis, 'I cannot recall'

Finally, how to persuade an inquiry
What you say is the true history
Tho' the transcripts will later show
A puzzle, cloaked in smoke, shrouded in mystery …

- Graeme

Only one nation to save

I welcome you as your Governor
Hence, my colourful regalia
Founded in 1788, the mighty nation
Of New South Wale-Straya

I'm Admiral Arthur Phillip Morrison
And without a hint of malice
Here's my Chancellor of the Injector
Loyal Gold-Standard Gladys

I have a serious announcement
Here in Cronulla Great Hall
A foreign plague has landed
A virus trying to kill us all

Yes, other outposts are suffering
Such as that madman in the West
Who via his Auslan interpreter
Beats his fists on his Laborite chest

And we hear the drums a'beating
With vitriol spewing forth
From the Loudmouthed Loony Lefties
Of The Blistering Sunny North

Not forgetting to the south of us
Led by that prickly political piranha
Dan's obscure little whinging mob
Stuffy old Victoriana

Come On Victoria! I'm Done.

But, New South Wale-Straya
Is the true Antipodean nation
Founded on courage, love and guns
And a land-grabbing citation

As the situation is now serious
Becoming a truly deadly race
Kidnap the very best doctors
Put the very best practice in place

Send the troops across the borders
To steal everyone's vaccines
Round up every testing kit
Purloin ventilating machines

You can trust me, Admiral Morrison
In my very best regalia
There's only one land worth saving now
And that is New South Wale-Straya

- Graeme

Twenty days of footy heaven

I am beside myself with glee
My eyes are all ablaze
Set for thirty-three footy games
In just twenty COVID days

I fear potential injury
With play at such full throttle
Like the prospect of RSI
From opening all those bottles

Or getting fingers jammed
In the wonky bar-fridge door
Or losing the remote somewhere
Around table, couch or floor

Buggering up instructions
When recording a vital match
Discovering that you've taped
'How Pelicans Learn To Hatch'

It's a footy fest with all its lows
And moments of elation
So stay calm between matches
By practicing levitation

Change clothes once a week
A shower might help too
And eat plenty of sustaining food
Like dumplings in Irish stew

Turn yourself off Facebook
A smart thing, anyway
Let in the odd ray of sunlight
So your skin won't fade to grey

Come On Victoria! I'm Done.

Now, buckle up fans
With every ounce of endurance
Drink lots of water
And check your health insurance ...

- Graeme

Locked out of the sunshine

Our bags are packed, we're off to Queensland
It's too cold here, we're sniffing and sneazlin'
Winter in Melbourne is far too chilly to stay here
We're heading up north where we fritter time away there
Until the sun comes back down to Capricorn
Then it's too hot for comfort so we head back home
The summer clothes have been washed and ironed
The caravan is hooked up, the wheels realigned
The house is clean and the dog is safely in the back
Nothing left to do, nothing left to pack
Hang on
What's this, what's wrong?
The borders are shut, they won't let us through!
They don't want Victorians, what are we to do?
They reckon we carry the coronavirus
They've hung us out to dry before they even tried us
I'm as mad as hell, all anger and ire
It's a staycation for us in front of the fire

- Elsie

Come **O**n **V**ictoria! **I**'m **D**one.

The Olympics in Tokyo

It was 2020 and the world had heard plenty
About the virus that was running amuck
Japan had invested in venues untested
But somehow had run out of luck
Everything was ready but ceased and stood steady
Because the world was living in fear
The Olympic spirit dampened, the virus was rampant
There would be no games in Tokyo this year

Come 2021, they did a rerun, world athletes heeded the call
Competitive and keen, young, fit and lean, all for one and one for all
Athletes from Australia to Uzbekistan swam, soared,
jumped and ran
At home we became experts on every sport and game plan
As we watched it enthralled,
on the new big television we had installed
We cheered for our teams and individuals as well
When a medal was won, we felt our hearts swell
For the young folk who strove to be best at whatever the test
And who made Lockdown 6 brighter and all our hearts lighter
Thank you

- Elsie

We're over it, Dan!

The rules, the flaming rules, shut down the child-care centres and the schools,
Don't have family in your home, wear a mask when you walk but not when you run
We're over it! We've had enough! We're done!
Draconian rules and prohibitions
Coupled with meaningless restrictions
Home schooling, working with child on the knee
Cranky teenagers, desperate unemployed dads, a sure fire recipe
For family violence and poor mental health outcomes
The burden falls upon families, but mostly on the Mums
Fly football players round the country
but ban children in playgrounds
Rules for one and not the other and silly as it sounds
They thought it would stop parents in parks milling about
At the end of a day's home schooling when kids are finally let out
And at the same time the politicians were negotiating
For construction sites to operate and sports crowds promoting
Inconsistent pandemic rules application
Lack transparency and justification
'We can show New South Wales,'
determined the power-hungry men
'We will determine how Victorians will live and when
'You will not be released from the COVID burden
'It can't be that bad, we're not hurting
'Business and workers may well be
'But we aim to eradicate this virus completely'
Such ignorant disconnect from reality
As it turned out, the politicians were wrong, the battle can't be won

Come On Victoria! I'm Done.

Why did Victoria think we could do what
nobody in the world has done?
Did Daniel Andrews and his vainglorious cohorts
Dream arrogantly of victory over nature's powerful force
In the end, all the huffing and puffing amounted to nought
The virus wins and has its way
It is its own juggernaut

- Elsie

The new look Games

Welcome everyone, to the new look Games
Where performers have gathered to seek medals and fame
But it's a rejigged Olympics in this challenging year
Where records broken may not be cherished I fear

You see, the 100 metres sprint is now totally new
It's based on coming first in a vaccination queue
So guile and strategy is required as much as speed
Persuading a young medico is the skill that you need

And the usual method of giving a jab is unravelling
Think of what can be delivered by an AstraZeneca javelin
And there is a new event, just sitting on an exerciser
Pedalling while you wait, and wait, and wait for a Pfizer

The marathon has been given a neat modification
It's for lasting longest in a car outside a testing station
So, no longer a foot race against the ever-ticking clock
You win by driving around and around and around the block

Weightlifters don't have to bother using weights
They lift the vaccination vials in their delivery crates
And a new removalists event combines strength and drama
Delivering an upright piano from Kyoto to Yokohama

Of course, we will be vigilant, and take anyone to task
Who cheats by daring to wear an aerodynamic mask
Then there is the matter, of the banned equestrian, of course
Did he take the coke? Or did he give it to the horse ..?

- Graeme

Come On Victoria! I'm Done.

At last

El confinamiento
Feng cheng
Le confinement
Locked down the city, we were all compliant
We stayed home, venturing out for exercise or food
Pubs and schools closed, we work alone in solitude
Hospitals struggled
Services buckled
Our frontline workers were exhausted and spent
Amid an underlying tone of discontent
As the death toll soared
Our children became bored
Suffering from a truly psychological ordeal
Where nothing was on an even keel
Pandemic fatigue set in, loneliness, loss, anger, fear and more
Ended a sad and desolate year of body bag and empty store
We missed our old life and hated being alone
Silently suffering from isolation syndrome
Then, at last came the order from the leader of our nation
The miracle of the vaccination would end suspended animation
Collective smiles and sighs of relief
Mingled mourning for loss and grief
After months of false dawns and isolation
We embraced freedom with optimism
Let's move on, banish this memory, celebrate life today
While the sun shines, let's make hay

- Elsie

The authors

ELSIE and Graeme Johnstone are husband and wife, living in a Bayside suburb of Melbourne, writing both individually and as a team on a variety of projects including novels, histories, memoirs, musicals and poems.

Elsie was originally a primary school teacher and special education specialist, while Graeme had a long and successful career in country, suburban and daily newspaper journalism.

In 1998, they quit their jobs and set up The Wordsmith's Shop, a unique establishment that wrote everything from personal letters to books for a wide range of clients.

This also gave them the chance to move into the more creative world of writing.

Come **O**n **V**ictoria! **I**'m **D**one.

More books

Elsie

Our Little Town, Growing Up in Lakes Entrance
Ma's Garden
Around the Kitchen Table
Rainbow Over Narre Warren
Lakes Entrance girl - Collected poems
Catholic girl – Collected poems

Graeme

The Playmakers
Joan, Child of Labor
OK Boomer and other radio poems
Chardonnay Socialist and other radio poems
Skase, Spain & Me (Tony Larkins)

Elsie and Graeme

Lover, Husband, Father, Monster
Book 1, Her Story
Book 2, His Story
Book 3, The Aftermath

All books available in paperback or e-book via Amazon and other outlets.

www.ingramcontent.com/pod-product-compliance
Lightning Source LLC
Chambersburg PA
CBHW050321010526
44107CB00055B/2345